WONDERFUL
WYOMING

FACTS and FOODS

Judy Barbour

Dedicated to

the wonderful state of Wyoming and all of the people who have
contributed to its greatness; and especially to all of the wonderful
friends that I have made through the years.

also

with love to my wonderful husband, Barry, whose contributions
to this book have been many; to my loving sons, Donald and
Barry Gorden and my beautiful little helper, my little grand-
daughter, Susan Poole Barbour.

Printed in the United States of America

First Printing May, 1989

PUBLISHER
Judy Barbour Books
2305 Park Avenue
Bay City, Texas 77414

Introduction

Wyoming is truly one of the most beautiful places in the world! When you see it, life will never be the same again.

Millions come from all over the world to enjoy the many pleasures this magnificent state has to offer — hunting, fishing, boating, floating the river, riding the rapids, mountain climbing, hiking, camping out, biking, horseback riding, skiing, sleighing, dog sledding, picnicking, photographing, sightseeing, shopping, as well as going to rodeos, absorbing museums, galleries of western art, Indian reservations, trading posts, being a cowboy, honky-tonking, dude ranching, watching the beautiful sunrise and sunset, breathing the fresh, invigorating air, just thinking — have I left anything out? Each is an enchanting new discovery that continually lures you to the West! Nature provides the entertainment, you partake of the magnificence.

In your discovery of this unique state, you will learn about the history, the people and the contributions of a special breed — those with a great spirit of adventure, courage and pride.

You may leave and return to your own lifestyle, but within your heart remains a piece of this great state and way of life, and you shall return again, if only in your dreams; yet once you have experienced the magic of Wyoming, you shall never be the same!

May you enjoy!

Judy

Judy Barbour

Wonderful Wyoming

Wyoming is an exciting and adventurous Rocky Mountain state with beautiful scenery and enormous natural resources. Even the name, the Delaware Indian word meaning "upon the great plain," has an exciting ring to it.

Geographically, it is one of the most beautiful and unspoiled of the states, famous for its abundant, awesome natural resources — magnificent towering, snow-capped mountains, crystal clear peaceful lakes and mighty rivers with swirling white rapids; beautiful valleys, vast plains, abundant wildlife, fishes and fresh air — all wonders of the world! Millions of tourists from all over the world visit Wyoming each year for its recreational areas, historic sites and magnificent scenery.

Wyoming has the distinction of being a "man-made" state — a nearly perfect rectangle with no "natural" boundaries. In all of the United States, there are only four states with completely artificial boundaries. It was the 44th state to join the Union, on July 10, 1890, and it is the ninth largest in territory (fourth largest of the Rocky Mountain states). With 480,000 plus people, Wyoming ranks 49th in population. Millions of people have gone to Wyoming, but few have stayed.

The characteristics of the land are unique. Wyoming lies where the Great Plains meet the Rocky Mountains. The Continental Divide, which separates the United States, winds its way through Wyoming from the rugged mountains of the northwest to the south-central edge of the state. Atlantic Creek and Pacific Creek originate less than a quarter mile apart, yet their waters go in opposite directions to two mighty oceans separated by thousands of miles. Wyoming is indeed, physically, a land of contrasts.

The history of Wyoming is so important, intriguing and interesting, that one would benefit greatly by reading extensively on the subject. A concise condensation follows, with noteworthy historical facts highlighted throughout these pages.

The people, places and events that have made the history of Wyoming are monumental. It is a land of discovery of vast natural and human resources. It is believed that the first inhabitants of Wyoming were prehistoric Indian hunters of 11,000 or more years ago; however, little is known about the ancient civilization. Later, large herds of buffalo roamed the prairies. The Indians prized them for their food, as well as for their hides.

Since the 16th century, a number of governments have claimed parts of what is now Wyoming. Many flags have flown over the Wyoming territory: the United States, Great Britain, Spain, France, Mexico and Texas; also the territories of Louisiana, Utah, Dakotas, Idaho, Oregon, Washington, Missouri and Nebraska.

Chronologically, the history of Wyoming was shaped by many people and events. All came to pursue the vast frontier — in search of a new land, new life and new opportunity. The first trailblazers were explorers, trappers and fur traders. Some of the first were Spanish explorers of the 1500s and 1600s. French trappers may have come in the early 1700s; however, exploration did not begin until after 1800 when the United States bought the area from France as a part of the Louisiana Purchase, resulting in the Lewis and Clark Expedition. Numerous important discoveries followed, with a trapper named John Coulter being the first white man to see Yellowstone Park in 1807. Beaver hats were quite fashionable for stylish Europeans and affluent Americans, so when trappers found rich pelts in the Wyoming area, this discovery opened Wyoming to the modern world.

During the 1820s and '30s, fur trade became more specialized, with the first rendezvous (gathering) of trappers organized by General William Ashley in 1824 for the purpose of trading ammunition, food and other supplies for furs. The yearly rendezvous became important to trappers, not only for trading, but also as a social occasion and an anticipated time to exchange news.

Next came those in search of a new life as the westward movement became important in the 1820s. Gold was discovered in California in 1849, resulting in an even greater westward movement through Wyoming. There were great battles between the white man and the Indians. With the advent of the railroad in 1867, boomtowns sprang up all along the route. Many were quickly gone; however, many flourished. The effect the railroad had on Wyoming was incredible, and when it was completed, Wyoming was only a few days away from either coast. Thus, Wyoming became an important link in American history.

One of the most outstanding historical accomplishments of great significance in the entire world was in 1869, when the territory of Wyoming became the first government in the *world* to give equal rights to women.

The destiny of Wyoming was further shaped, after the Civil War, when cattle drives from Texas to the north and east began. Wyoming was excellent cattle country, so an era of cowboys, cattlemen and outlaws followed. Sheep ranching also dominated.

A great period of Wyoming settlement did not come until the 1880s. Times were hard, but happy, in the land that was rough, rugged and wild. Wyoming became a state in 1890 and the frontier was gone. Now, one hundred years later, in 1990, the Wyoming Centennial is celebrated! Tourism became important in the early 1900s as President Theodore Roosevelt designated Devil's Tower as the first national monument in 1906. Wyoming's oil boom began in 1912 and is only one of the state's rich natural resources that were later discovered. These include oil, natural gas, coal, trona, uranium, bentonite, soda ash and agriculture. Wyoming's economy boomed during World War II as the war brought great demands for the state's resources. Economic development continued after the war and tourism increased.

Between 1970 and 1980, the population of Wyoming grew by 42%, one of the highest in the nation. Many came to work in its mining industries.

Wyoming is an abundant state with much to contribute — all gifts of nature. It has transformed from a "wild and woolly," cowboys-and-Indians state to a state of sophistication, yet the magical aura and lure of the West prevail. The wonders and magnitude of its natural treasures are for all to cherish, preserve and enjoy.

The foods of Wyoming and the West were neither fancy nor sophisticated; just hearty, substantial fare to sustain those early people. The first inhabitants of Wyoming, the early Indians, explorers and trappers, lived off the land on the abundant source of buffalo, wild game and fish, supplemented with wild berries, morels and other native plants. Next, those traveling west were urged to carry enough staples on the wagon trains, such as flour, baking soda, sugar, lard, black pepper, baking powder, coffee and molasses to supplement the resources of game and fish. The fur traders traded for foods.

As Wyoming became more settled, the new settlers often had a cow or two, some chickens and also planted gardens, thus more variety of foods became available. With the beginning of the cattle and sheep industry, Wyoming became a big meat state. Finally, as the railroad was completed, there was greater access to more foods. Early Wyoming cooks were resourceful, using what they had.

I have chosen a selection of foods reflective of the land from whence it came, yet practical and appropriate for today's life style. Let the adventure begin!

Important Facts About
WYOMING

Capital	Cheyenne
State Motto	"Equal Rights"
Nickname	Equality State Cowboy State
Statehood	July 10, 1890 — 44th state
Size	97,914 square miles — 9th largest
Highest Point	13,804 feet, Gannett Peak, Wind River Range
Lowest Point	3,100 feet, near Belle Fourche River
Mean Elevation	6,100 feet, second highest in the nation
State Symbol	Bucking horse and rider (on license plate since 1936)
State Song	"Wyoming" — words by Charles E. Winter, music by G. E. Knapp
State Flower	Indian Paintbrush
State Bird	Western Meadow Lark
State Tree	Cottonwood
State Fish	Salmo Clarki (Cutthroat Trout)
State Mammal	Bison
State Gem	Jade (Nephrite)
First and Largest National Park	Yellowstone, established in 1872
First National Monument	Devil's Tower, established in 1906
First National Forest	Shoshone — first ever designated in the world

Contents

Something Special ...

Appetizers, Salads, Vegetables
Fondues, Drinks

The "first discoverer," trapper John Coulter, came to Wyoming as an explorer with the Lewis and Clark Expedition. He was the first to discover Yellowstone Park in 1807. He was among the first to see the Snake River, Big Horn and Wind River Ranges, Teton Mountains and Jackson Hole.

Buffalo Burgundy-Bacon Meatballs

24 slices bacon
1 pound ground buffalo
    (or beef, elk, deer, moose)
3 tablespoons onion, minced
2 tablespoons parsley, minced
1 cup Burgundy wine
1 cup fresh bread crumbs
1 egg, beaten
salt and pepper to taste
1 teaspoon dry mustard
½ teaspoon Italian seasonings
hot mustard

Partially cook bacon and drain. Mix together meat, onion, parsley, one-half cup wine, bread crumbs, egg, salt, pepper, dry mustard and Italian seasonings. Shape into one-inch balls. Wrap in bacon slices that have been halved crosswise. Secure with toothpicks.

Bake at 375 degrees for 20 to 25 minutes until bacon is crisp. Drain. Place in chafing dish with remaining one-half cup Burgundy. Serve with hot mustard dip.

In 1812, Robert Stuart discovered South Pass through the Rocky Mountains. This important discovery enabled those traveling west to have easy access through the mountains and opened the way to what later became the great westward movement of the Oregon Trail. Three of the monumental pioneer trails of the American West took their covered wagons through South Pass; those of the California, Mormon and Oregon Trails.

Smoked Rocky Mountain Trout Log

8 ounces smoked rainbow trout
8 ounces cream cheese, softened
1 tablespoon lemon juice
2 tablespoons onion, grated
1 teaspoon prepared horseradish
dash salt
½ cup pecans, chopped
2 tablespoons fresh parsley, chopped

Combine cream cheese, lemon juice, onion, horseradish and salt. Gently stir in fish and mix thoroughly. Chill several hours. Combine pecans and parsley. Shape fish mixture into log shape. Roll in mixture of nuts and parsley. Serve with crackers. Yield: 3 cups

12

The first annual rendezvous (gathering) of trappers was established in 1824, on the Green River, by General William Ashley for the purpose of trading ammunition, food and other supplies for furs. The yearly rendezvous was eagerly anticipated not only for trading, but also as a social occasion and a time to exchange news. It was certainly the most famous social event of the trapping era!

Jerky

Cut deer, elk or beef mixture into ¼-inch thick strips. Place in 2-quart glass dish. Layer meat, sprinkling the following in order:

Baste with liquid smoke, extra-fine granulated sugar, Lowry's seasoned salt, coarse pepper, onion and garlic powder and sugar cured (natural smoke flavor).

Cover and let set in refrigerator overnight. Place strips on foil-covered cookie sheet. Place in 200-degree oven. Cook 4 hours, turn and cook 4 more hours. Store in airtight containers.

Homemade Salami

2 pounds lean ground beef, elk, moose, deer
**   or buffalo**
1 cup water
¼ teaspoon each onion powder and coarse
**   ground black pepper**
½ teaspoon garlic powder
1 tablespoon liquid smoke
2½ tablespoons meat cure salt
2 tablespoons mustard seed

Combine and mix gently all ingredients. Shape into three rolls 2 inches in diameter. Wrap each in foil. Refrigerate 24 hours. When ready to cook, pierce the bottom side of each roll with a fork. Place rolls, pierced side down, on broiler pan over pan of 2 to 3 cups water. Bake at 325 degrees for 1½ hours. Serve warm or cold.

Oil was discovered in the Wind River mountain area by Captain Benjamin L. E. Bonneville in 1833 and was first used for axle grease. Oil has been one of Wyoming's most important natural resources.

Duck Breast Tidbits with Wild Game Dip*

duck breasts, deboned and cubed into
 bite-sized pieces.
1 orange, juiced
½ cup white wine
¼ cup teriyaki sauce
3 tablespoons sherry
½ cup green onions with tops, sliced
½ cup fresh parsley, chopped
bacon, sliced crosswise into thirds

Marinate duck breast cubes in marinade of orange juice, white wine, teriyaki sauce, sherry, green onions and parsley for several hours. Wrap in bacon slices and secure with a toothpick.

Roast over charcoal hibachi or in oven broiler in marinade until bacon is crisp, turning several times. Serve with wild game dip.

*Equally delicious with chicken breasts!

Wild Game Dip

2 cups apricot preserves
¼ cup fresh lemon juice
½ cup white wine
2 tablespoons teriyaki sauce
¼ teaspoon cayenne pepper
salt and pepper to taste

In saucepan, combine apricot preserves, lemon juice, wine, teriyaki sauce, cayenne pepper, salt and pepper. Stir until well blended. Cook and reduce to thicken. Yield: 1½ to 2 cups.

This is an excellent accompaniment to all wild game dishes!

In 1834, traders William Sublette and Robert Campbell established Fort William (later Fort Laramie). It was the area's first trading post. In 1849, the United States took it over to protect the travelers who migrated west in pioneer wagon trains on the trails against the Indians. Many buildings and ruins remain here and have been superbly restored.

Beef or Venison Kebabs

2 pounds elk, deer or beef steaks, sliced across the grain, diagonally, into paper-thin strips (4-inch by 1-inch by ¼-inch)
¾ cup vegetable oil
¾ cup sesame oil
⅔ cup soy or teriyaki sauce
⅔ cup dry sherry
⅔ cup brown sugar
¼ teaspoon dry mustard
2 cloves garlic
1 to 1½ teaspoons red chili peppers, crushed

Mix oils, soy sauce, sherry, brown sugar, mustard, garlic and crushed red pepper into a marinade. Pour into a shallow pan, add strips of meat and turn to coat evenly. Cover and refrigerate at least 2 hours, turning to coat.

Interlace strips of meat in ribbon fashion on bamboo skewers. (Soak skewers in water prior to using to prevent burning.) Brush meat heavily with marinade.

Cook on hibachi or grill over hot coals until done, approximately 5 minutes, turning to brown evenly. Baste with marinade while cooking. Yield: 18 to 20 appetizers.

Fort Bridger was established as the second permanent settlement in Wyoming in 1843 by Jim Bridger, a very colorful, famous trapper, explorer, hunter, guide and scout that blazed trails all across the Rocky Mountains and contributed greatly to the exploration of Wyoming.

Wyoming Beef Pinwheels

3 pounds flank steak (2 steaks)
2 tablespoons fresh red bell pepper or
    pimientos, chopped
⅓ cup Parmesan cheese, grated
2 tablespoons fresh parsley, chopped
2 tablespoons Dijon mustard
½ teaspoon black pepper
salt and coarse ground black pepper to taste
3 tablespoons oil
2 cloves garlic, minced
parsley, chopped

Mix together red bell pepper or pimiento, Parmesan cheese, parsley, mustard and pepper to blend. Spread over one side of each steak, dividing evenly. Roll lengthwise, tightly, jelly-roll style. Season with salt and pepper to taste. Place seam side down and cut into 1-inch thick slices to yield 24.

Thread on bamboo skewers (previously soaked in water, so they do not burn). Mix together oil and garlic and brush pinwheels. Grill or broil until done. Sprinkle with additional chopped parsley. Yield: 24 appetizers.

In the mid 1800s, Mormons crossed the plains by the thousands in search of the promised land on the shores of the Great Salt Lake where they could have a new life free from persecution. At one time, there were as many as 16,000 Mormons traveling in Wyoming; the largest single migration in the country's history.

Star Valley Cheese Ball

1 cup Star Valley Cheddar cheese, grated
1 cup Star Valley Swiss cheese, grated
1 cup Mexican Velveeta cheese, grated
1 cup Monterey Jack cheese with jalapenos, grated
8 ounces cream cheese, softened
½ cup Miracle Whip
½ cup green onions with tops, finely chopped
¼ cup Spanish olives, pimiento-stuffed, chopped
2 tablespoons sweet pickle relish
½ cup pecans, finely chopped
salt and pepper to taste
¼ cup fresh parsley, snipped

Let cheeses soften to room temperature. Combine all cheeses and add salad dressing. Add green onions, olives, pickle relish and one-half of the pecans. Season with salt and pepper. Blend well and chill. Shape into a large ball. Roll in remaining nuts and parsley and dust with paprika. Serve chilled with assorted crackers. Yield: One cheese ball.

The first school in Wyoming was founded in 1852 at Fort Laramie by William Vaux, the chaplain of the fort.

Indian Eggs

6 hard-boiled eggs, shelled
1 cup canned beet juice
1 cup cider vinegar
1 clove garlic, crushed
½ bay leaf
salt and pepper to taste

Place eggs carefully in a large heat-proof glass jar. Combine remaining ingredients, bring to a boil and pour over eggs. Cover, cool and refrigerate about 8 hours. Yield: 6 eggs.

Hot and Spicy Fireside Dip

16-ounce can jellied cranberry sauce
3 tablespoons prepared horseradish
2 tablespoons honey
1 tablespoon Worchestershire sauce
1 tablespoon lemon juice
1 clove garlic, minced
½ teaspoon ground red pepper
orange segments
pineapple tidbits
miniature smoked sausages, browned

Heat together in a saucepan cranberry sauce, horseradish, honey, Worchestershire sauce, lemon juice, garlic and red pepper. Place in serving dish and serve warm with oranges, pineapple and sausages on toothpicks for dipping. Yield: 1½ cups.

The need for transcontinental connections brought the Pony Express in 1860 to carry the mail from St. Joseph, Missouri to San Francisco as quickly as possible. The route across Wyoming followed that of the Oregon Trail to South Pass then to Salt Lake City. The Pony Express was dangerous yet glamourous, and although it only lasted 16 short months until the transcontinental telegraph was completed in 1861, it provided not only a way to get the mail to its destination faster, but also provided the vital link between East and West.

Indian Summer Picnic Pate´

4 tablespoons butter
½ pound fresh mushrooms, sliced
1 pound chicken livers
1 teaspoon each garlic salt and paprika
⅓ cup green onions with tops, finely chopped
⅓ cup white wine
3 drops Tabasco
½ cup butter, softened
salt

Simmer in a skillet for 5 minutes in 4 tablespoons of butter: mushrooms, chicken livers, garlic, salt, paprika and green onions. Add white wine and Tabasco and cook slowly 5 to 10 minutes more. Cool and whirl in a blender. Blend in additional ½ cup butter and salt to taste. Place in an oiled 3-cup decorative mold and chill. (Paté will be thin prior to chilling.) Unmold and serve with toast points or crackers. Yield: 3 cups.

The Bozeman Trail, pioneered in 1863 as a shortcut to the Montana gold camps, cuts north from the Oregon Trail near Douglas and is close to Buffalo and Sheridan. It became known as "the bloody Bozeman" because of the anger and violence that triggered the Sioux Indian raids as they tried to maintain their last great hunting ground.

Picnic Olive-Egg Salad

6 hard-boiled eggs, chopped
½ cup celery, finely diced
¼ cup Spanish olives, pimiento-stuffed, chopped
⅓ cup mayonnaise
1 tablespoon prepared mustard
salt and pepper to taste

Combine all ingredients and mix well.

Ruby Red Fruit Compote

1 honeydew melon, seeds removed and shaped into balls
½ pint fresh raspberries
½ pint fresh strawberries, hulled
½ pound bing cherries, stemmed and pitted
4 cups watermelon balls
½ to 1 cup Champagne
fresh mint, garnish

Combine all fruits in a large bowl. Add Champagne and stir gently to combine. Refrigerate to chill, tossing occasionally, to coat evenly with Champagne. Serve in a pretty glass bowl, garnished with fresh mint, as a salad or dessert choice. Serves 6.

In 1867, the Union Pacific Railroad began construction in Wyoming. It had tremendous impact in shaping the growth, development and future of the state. With the arrival of the railroad, many "Hell on Wheels" boomtowns sprang up. Cheyenne was first, then Laramie, Rawlins, Green River and Evanston, as well as other short-lived ones. Towns literally sprang up overnight, acquiring thousands of citizens — with a rough and rowdy way of life. When the railroad was completed, resulting in Wyoming's accessibility to and from either coast, a new era began.

Ranch Slaw

6 cups green cabbage, finely shredded
2 cups purple cabbage, finely shredded
1 green bell pepper, chopped
3 carrots, grated
1 onion, finely chopped
¾ cup white vinegar
⅔ cup sugar
⅔ cup oil
1 teaspoon salt
1 teaspoon celery seeds
1 teaspoon dry mustard

Combine cabbages, green bell pepper, carrots and onion in a large bowl. Place remaining ingredients in a saucepan. Bring to a boil. Pour hot liquid over cabbage mixture. Cool and refrigerate several hours to allow flavors to blend. Serves 8.

In 1868, the Wind River Indian Reservation was presented to Chief Washakie, a great world leader and chief of the Shoshone nation for almost 50 years, by the United States government. Fort Washakie is the only remaining Indian Reservation in Wyoming today. The name, "Washakie," means "gourd rattle."

Baked Stuffed Potatoes

4 large Idaho potatoes
1½ cups milk
4 tablespoons butter
salt and pepper to taste
¼ pound bacon, fried crisp and crumbled
3 tablespoons chives, minced
¼ cup Parmesan cheese, grated
1½ cups Cheddar cheese, grated

Bake potatoes at 400 degrees for 1½ hours or until done. Cut in half, lengthwise, and scoop out potatoes, reserving shells. Whip potatoes with milk, butter, salt and pepper. Fold in bacon and chives. Spoon potato mixture back into shells. Top with mixed cheeses and paprika. Put in baking dish and bake in hot oven, for 5 to 10 minutes, until cheese is bubbly. Serves 6 to 8.

Marinated Onions

4 white or red onions, medium-size,
**   peeled and sliced, separated into rings**
¾ cup each sugar and salad oil
¼ cup vinegar
½ teaspoon salt
1/8 teaspoon cracked pepper

Cover onions with cold water. Let stand one hour, changing water every 15 minutes. (This takes the bite out of the onions.) Drain. Mix remaining ingredients. Place in 2-quart bowl. Chill 24 hours, stirring occasionally. Yield: 2 cups.

Delicious accompaniment to meat dishes!

*Wyoming is most widely known as the "Equality State." It was the first government in the **world** to give equal right to vote to women in 1869. Ester Hobart Morris became the first woman justice of the peace in 1870 and is known as "The Mother of Women's Suffrage!"*

Glazed Carrots

2 pound carrots
3 tablespoons butter
2 tablespoons brown sugar
¼ cup fresh orange juice
2 tablespoons orange marmalade

Wash and scrape carrots. Cut carrots on the diagonal in 1- to 2-inch pieces. Cook, uncovered (to preserve color), in a small amount of boiling water for 5 minutes. Reduce heat, add butter, brown sugar, orange juice and orange marmalade and cook 8 to 10 minutes, just until tender-crisp and carmelized. Stir frequently to prevent burning. Serves 8.

Garden Fresh Green Beans

2 tablespoons butter or margarine, melted
¼ cup green onions with tops, sliced
¼ cup green bell pepper, chopped
¼ cup celery with leaves, chopped
4 cups fresh green beans, snapped
¼ cup diced smoked ham
salt and pepper to taste
dash garlic powder
2 to 3 dashes Tabasco
3 tablespoons toasted almonds
½ cup red bell pepper, finely chopped

Saute green onions, bell peppers, and celery in butter. Add green beans and steam until tender-crisp. Add ham and seasonings. Toss to mix. Add almonds and red bell peppers and toss again. Serve immediately. Serves 6 to 8.

Yellowstone National Park is one of the most immense and magnificent scenic areas on earth. Located in northwestern Wyoming, as well as in parts of Idaho and Montana, it encompasses some 2 million acres of land and is the nation's oldest and largest national park, established in 1872. It has some of the most fascinating sights and spectacular formations found anywhere in the world, including unique geysers such as Old Faithful (the most famous), hot springs and waterfalls.

Baked Acorn Squash

4 small acorn squash
2 tablespoons butter
brown sugar
cinnamon

Cut tops off each squash. Steam, cut side down in covered pot, in a small amount of water, for 20 minutes. Carefully remove; scoop out squash, mash and combine with butter. Fill shells with mixture, top each with brown sugar and sprinkle with cinnamon. Bake at 350 degrees for 10 to 15 minutes. Serves 4.

Indian Corn Pudding

24 ounces corn niblets
3 eggs, lightly whipped
1 pint half-and-half
salt and pepper to taste
½ stick butter, cut into small pieces

Combine corn, eggs and half-and-half. Season to taste with salt and pepper. Pour into buttered 2-quart casserole and dot top with butter. Bake at 350 degrees for 30 minutes. Test for doneness by inserting knife in center of pudding. When done, knife will come out clean. Serves 6.

The Wyoming state seal was adopted in 1893. On the seal, the woman and the motto symbolize equal rights of women in the state. The two men are representative of the importance of the state's livestock and mining industries. The dates are those on which Wyoming became a territory and a state.

Stuffed Tomato Cups

Tomatoes are a *fruit* that America gave the world!

4 fresh tomatoes, medium
10-ounce package frozen peas and onions
salt and pepper to taste
butter

Cut a ¼-inch slice from top of each tomato. Hollow-out tomatoes, leaving shells intact. Chop pulp and tops and reserve.

Pour boiling water over peas and onions in a bowl. Let set one minute, drain and toss with reserved tomato bits. Salt and pepper inside of tomato cups. Fill with vegetable mixture. Place in ovenproof dish and dot with butter. Bake at 375 degrees for 15 minutes. Serves 4.

Round Up Three-Bean Salad

1 (15½-ounce) can each: kidney beans,
 cut green beans and wax beans
4-ounce can mushrooms, drained
15½-ounce can artichoke hearts, drained
 and quartered
7-ounce can ripe olives, drained and sliced
12-ounce can corn, drained
1 purple onion, sliced thin and separated
 into rings
Dressing: **⅔ cup oil**
   ¼ cup each dry red wine and
    cider vinegar
   ½ cup bell pepper, chopped finely
   salt and pepper to taste
   1 teaspoon prepared mustard

Combine all salad ingredients. Blend dressing ingredients and pour over salad. Chill several hours, stirring to blend. Serves 12 to 15.

Laramie, named for the French-Canadian trapper, Jacques La Ramee, is the third largest city in Wyoming. It is the home of the state's only four-year institution of higher learning, the University of Wyoming, founded in 1886. The state is very proud of its University of Wyoming Cowboys!

Swiss Cheese Fondue

1 split clove garlic
1 pound Swiss cheese, diced
3 tablespoons flour
2 cups dry white wine
1 tablespoon lemon juice
3 tablespoons Kirsch (cherry liqueur)
dash nutmeg, pepper and paprika
2 loaves French bread, cut into cubes, with
      crust left on
vegetable crudites: broccoli and cauliflower
      flowerettes, carrot and celery sticks,
      steamed Brussels sprouts, cherry
      tomatoes, etc.

Dredge cheese with flour. Rub fondue pot with garlic, add wine and place over moderate heat. Do not boil. When wine is hot, add lemon juice, then add flour-dredged cheese, a handful at a time. Bring mixture to a bubble for an instant. Add Kirsch and spices, until blended. Serve in fondue, earthenware or chafing dish over sterno heat. Spear bread cubes and crudites and swirl in the melted cheese mixture. Serves 4.

On July 10, 1890, Wyoming became the 44th state to join the Union. It is 9th in territory and 49th in population, with 480,000 people.

Meat Fondue

**2 pounds assorted meats, cubed or bite-size:
    beef, chicken, lobster, shrimp, scallops,
    or game meats
½ pound butter
⅔ cup corn or peanut oil**

Combine butter and oil in a fondue pot (stainless steel for high heat) over sterno. Spear a cube of meat with fondue fork and cook in hot butter/oil mixture until done to one's taste. Cook ½ minute for rare, 1 minute for medium and 2 minutes for well done. Dip into sauce of your choice.

Hot Mustard Fondue Sauce

**2 teaspoons dry mustard
1 teaspoon warm water
¾ cup soy sauce**

Mix together dry mustard and water to form a smooth paste. Blend soy sauce into mustard paste. Great fondue sauce for meats; also excellent with egg rolls or boiled shrimp.

Horseradish Fondue Sauce

**1 cup sour cream
6 tablespoons horseradish
¼ cup onion, minced
¼ teaspoon black pepper**

Combine all ingredients in small bowl until well blended. Chill and serve with meat selections.

With the influx of homesteaders to Wyoming, feuds began between the large ranchers and the "nesters" and cattle rustlers. One of the most outstanding events in Wyoming history occurred in 1892 and was known as the Johnson County Cattle War as the big cattle ranchers took matters into their own hands following a dispute over cattle rustling.

Huckleberry Jam

4 cups crushed huckleberries
3 cups sugar

Crush huckleberries. Add sugar at a ratio of ¾ cup to 1 cup fruit. Stir over low heat until sugar dissolves, then bring to a rapid boil and stir constantly until jam is thick and a spoonful dropped onto a dish stays in place. The faster it thickens, the brighter the color and fresher the flavor.

Pour into hot, sterilized jars and seal immediately with melted wax or use metal lids and rings.

Chokecherry Syrup

1 pint chokecherry juice
3 cups sugar
½ cup light corn syrup

Make chokecherry juice by boiling chokecherries in just enough water to cover. Cook until berries are soft, then strain the juice through cheesecloth to yield 1 pint. Mix with sugar and corn syrup and simmer, uncovered, over low heat in heavy enamel or stainless steel pan about 15 minutes or until mixture is thick and syrupy. Serve over hot biscuits, waffles, freshly baked bread, plain cake or ice cream! Yield: 1 pint.

The historic Medicine Bow area was the setting for the western classic,
The Virginian, *well-known western novel by Owen Wister, published
in 1902. Dinosaur Graveyard, near Medicine Bow, is the site of
dinosaur fossil beds. Medicine Bow Ski Area is a haven for outdoor
enthusiasts.*

Alpine Glogg

1 liter red wine
2 cinnamon sticks
10 whole cloves
½ orange
½ lemon

Mix together, heat and remove from heat just as the mixture
starts to boil. Strain. Serve hot in mugs. Serves 4 to 6.

Snowmobiler's Spiced Tea

1 pound jar Tang
½ cup instant tea mix
1 teaspoon ground cinnamon
1 cup cinnamon red hots, crushed
1¼ cups sugar
½ cup lemonade mix
3-ounce package apricot gelatin

Combine all ingredients. Store in tightly closed jar. When
ready to use, measure according to taste in a mug of boiling
water.

Hot and Hearty ...

Main Dishes, Casseroles, Soups

In 1904, the Eaton Ranch, near Sheridan, became the first dude ranch in the West. Dude ranches offer the tourist one of the most enjoyable pleasures of the West.

Cowboy Steak

one 12-ounce beer
½ cup chili sauce
¼ cup salad oil
2 tablespoons soy sauce
1 tablespoon Dijon mustard
½ teaspoon Tabasco
1 medium onion, chopped coarsely
2 cloves garlic
3 pound sirloin steak (1½ to 2 inches thick)
salt and pepper to taste

Mix all ingredients except steak, salt and pepper; simmer 30 minutes. Brush steak with sauce.

Grill steak over medium-hot coals for 15 minutes on each side. Baste often with sauce. After turning, season to taste with salt and pepper. Serve with sauce. Yield: 8 servings.

Devil's Tower National Monument was established as the nation's first national monument by President Theodore Roosevelt in 1906. Located in the Black Hills Range in northeastern Wyoming, it is a spectacular volcanic tower that stands 865 feet above its base, which is 415 feet high.

Trout Hemingway, Barbour-Style

Ernest Hemingway was a great hunter and fisherman, so he knew and wrote of a good pan of fried trout. Simply speaking, there is nothing better than a freshly caught fried Rocky Mountan Trout; however, there are good ways and bad ways of preparing them. My version is perfect for cooking while camping out, or in the kitchen!

> 3 green onions with tops, finely chopped
> 1 tablespoon fresh parsley, minced
> juice of one lemon
> salt and pepper to taste
> 6 strips of bacon
> 6 freshly caught cut-throat or rainbow trout
>   (about 8 ounces each)
> ½ cup biscuit mix
> ¼ cup yellow cornmeal
> 1 teaspoon paprika
> lemon wedges, garnish

Combine green onions, parsley, lemon juice, salt and pepper and spread in cavities of fish. In a large frying pan, over medium heat, cook bacon crisp. Remove from pan. Drain.

Combine biscuit mix, cornmeal and paprika in a shallow pan. Carefully dredge both sides of trout in mixture. Cook fish in hot bacon grease until nicely browned, turning once. (For a 1-inch thick fish, allow 10 minutes total or 5 minutes per side.) Top each trout with bacon slice and garnish with lemon wedge. Serve with tartar sauce, if desired. Serves 6.

The beautiful red, white and blue Wyoming flag was adopted in 1917. It shows the state seal on a buffalo to symbolize the branding of livestock. Its red border symbolizes Indians, as well as the blood of pioneers.

Leg of Lamb of the West

5- to 6-pound leg of lamb
1 cup dry red wine
1 cup red wine vinegar and oil dressing
2 to 3 cloves garlic, slivered and pierced
    into meat at intervals
pepper to taste
2 onions, peeled and quartered
1 teaspoon Italian seasonings
1 teaspoon beef bouillon granules
2 tablespoons Worchestershire sauce
dash Tabasco
¼ cup soy sauce
dash paprika

Place leg of lamb and all other ingredients in roasting pan. Bake at 350 degrees for 2½ to 3 hours until meat is tender, basting frequently. (The secret is in the basting!) Skim off accumulated fat and serve juices with meat. Serves 8 to 10.

In 1920, Jackson became the first American town to be governed entirely by women. In 1924, Wyoming voters elected the first woman governor, Nellie Tayloe Ross. She was not only the first woman governor, but also later had the distinction of being the first woman director of the United States Mint.

Barry's Herb-Roasted Chicken With Vegetables

4 to 5 pound chicken
oil
sprinkling Italian seasonings
dash garlic salt
paprika
parsley
6 to 8 small potatoes, cut in half
4 medium carrots, cut in half-inch pieces
4 ribs celery, cut in half-inch pieces
14½-ounce can chicken broth
14½-ounce can beef broth

Rub chicken with oil. Sprinkle with seasonings. Place in large roaster and surround with vegetables. Add broths to level of one-third upon chicken, adding a small amount of water, if necessary.

Bake at 350 degrees, uncovered, for 1 hour, basting frequently. Cover, reduce heat to 250 degrees and bake an additional 45 minutes. Let cool 20 minutes (lid on), before serving. Serves 6 to 8.

In 1940 Wyoming celebrated 50 years of statehood. A commemorative anniversary stamp was issued by the United States government honoring this important event in history.

Steak Dianne

4 8-ounce each Filet Mignon steaks
coarsely ground black pepper
1 tablespoon oil
2½ tablespoons butter
1 clove garlic, pressed
2 tablespoons shallot bulbs, chopped
1 cup fresh mushrooms, sliced
2 tablespoons Worchestershire sauce
2 tablespoons red wine
½ teaspoon dry mustard
1 tablespoon fresh parsley, chopped
½ to ¾ cup brandy

Season steaks liberally with coarsely ground black pepper. Sear quickly over high heat in hot oil, approximately 1 to 1½ minutes per side. Remove from heat and cover to keep warm.

Melt butter in heavy skillet over moderate heat. Add garlic and shallot bulbs and cook 3 minutes. Add sliced mushrooms and cook an additional 2 minutes. Add Worchestershire sauce, red wine and mustard.

Add steaks, parsley and shallot tops. Cook 2 minutes, turning frequently. Turn heat up until fluid bubbles, then add brandy and ignite. Turn meat while flaming. When flame subsides, transfer steaks to serving plates, and pour sauce over each. Serves 4.

Great tableside presentation dinner!

About 1819, a party of French fur trappers camped at Pierre's Hole on the wetern, Idaho side of the magnificent mountain range. They named the three most prominent peaks "Les Trois Tetons" — the three breasts. Other names were given to the mountains by Indians and early explorers, but the French name won out. Grand Teton National Park, one of the most awesome, spectacular sights in North America, became a mini-park in 1929; however, it did not become a national park until 1950. It is located in northwestern Wyoming and includes the magnificent Teton mountain range, whose 7,000 foot cliffs rise like a gigantc stage set from the beautiful high mountain valley of Jackson Hole, just south of Yellowstone Park.

Baked Sage Hens or Grouse

2 sage hens or grouse (or chickens)
1 stick butter
seasoned salt and pepper
2 tablespoons Worchestershire sauce
dash Tabasco
1 onion, chopped
½ cup red wine vinegar
10-ounce can beef consomme
14½-ounce can beef bouillon
1 rib celery with leaves, chopped
1 green bell pepper, chopped

Rub birds with butter and sprinkle with seasoned salt and pepper. Place ½ stick butter in cavity of each. Combine all remaining ingredients. Place birds in roaster and add marinade. Cook, uncovered, at 350 degrees for 2 hours, basting frequently. Place lid on roaster and continue to cook an additional 1 hour. Turn oven up to 400 degrees and cook another 20 minutes. Serves 4 to 6.

The Teton Mountains are referred to as the "Cathedral Group;" the middle peak, or "Grand," is the tallest of the peaks at a height of 13,776 feet. The others are Mount Teewinot and Mount Owen.

Best of the West Veal

4 veal scallops, pounded paper-thin
flour
salt and pepper
6 tablespoons butter
2 tablespoons oil
3 tablespoons lemon juice
2 tablespoons fresh parsley, chopped
8 ounces green noodles or other pasta
lemon slices and parsley, garnish

Dust scallops with flour, salt and pepper. Heat 4 tablespoons butter with the oil in large skillet over medium-high heat until bubbly. Quickly brown scallops about 2 minutes per side. Remove to a warm platter and cover loosely.

Prepare noodles, cooking until just tender. Add lemon juice and parsley to skillet, remove from heat and add remaining butter.

Arrange scallops on noodles, top with butter sauce and garnish with lemon slices and additional parsley. Serves 2 and doubles with success.

The "Rocky Mountain Paradise," Jackson Hole, was made a national monument in 1950. The town of Jackson was named for Davey Jackson, a fur trapper who came to Wyoming in the early 1800s. This was his trapping "hole" — a secluded valley tucked between mountain ranges. It was Jackson's Hole and later became Jackson Hole. Eventually the name of the town was shortened to Jackson, with the entire valley being referred to as Jackson Hole.

Cheyenne Chicken

1 chicken, cut in serving pieces
salt, black pepper and cayenne pepper to taste
½ cup oil
1 pound fresh pork sausage links, sliced
1½ cups rice
2 large onions
½ cup green onions with tops, chopped
4 stalks of cerely with leaves, chopped
2 teaspoons garlic powder
½ cup fresh parsley, chopped
small can mushrooms
14½-ounce can each chicken and beef broth

Season chicken with salt, black pepper and cayenne pepper. Brown chicken in hot oil. Remove. Add rice to skillet, stirring to coat with oil. Remove from pan. Brown sausage in hot oil. Add vegetables into rice and saute. Add garlic powder parsley and mushrooms. Stir in broths and sausages.

Place rice and sausage mixture in a large rectangular ovenproof casserole dish. Arrange chicken pieces on top. Cover tightly with foil and bake at 350 degrees for 45 to 50 minutes. Add more broth if necessary. Uncover and cook an additional 20 to 30 minutes to brown. Yield: 6 servings.

The first settlers came to Jackson Hole in the late 1800s. Its economy was based on cattle for many years. Eventually, the scenery and big game hunting brought more visitors with summer tourism and skiing attracting many to the valley. Teton Village, with Rendezvous Peak, offers some of the most challenging skiing in America, with the highest vertical rise — 4,139 feet — in North America. Snow King Mountain, Jackson's oldest ski area, also offers fabulous skiing. Jackson has also become a mecca of western art and has the Wildlife of the American West Museum.

Barbecued Pork Loin

2- to 2½-pound pork loin
Marinade: 1½ **cups oil**
          ⅓ **cup red wine vinegar**
          2 **onions, chopped**
          ½ **cup chili sauce**
          1 **tablespoon brown sugar**
          2 **tablespoons Worchestershire**
            sauce
          1 **tablespoon chili powder**
          ½ **teaspoon each salt and pepper**
          2 **tablespoons Dijon mustard**

Mix all marinade ingredients together thoroughly. Place pork loin in deep dish. Pour marinade over to partially cover. Refrigerate 2 hours, turning occasionally to marinate thoroughly.

Remove meat from marinade and reserve marinade. Place loin on hot grill, cook 30 minutes per side for a total of one hour, basting frequently with reserve marinade. Insert meat thermometer in center of loin, at this time, to test. When internal temperature is 165 degrees, meat is done. Adjust cooking time accordingly. Serves 6 to 8.

*Sheridan is rich in history. In 1892 construction began on the lavish, opulent Sheridan Inn. It was the finest hotel between Chicago and San Francisco, modeled after an old world inn in Scotland. Southwest of Sheridan is the Bradford Brinton Memorial Ranch, near the settlement of Big Horn. It stands as a monument to the early day of Wyoming cattle barons and has an outstanding, valuable collection of art by well-known western artists. Among these is the **only** known painting of **Custer's Last Stand** by one of the most famous western artists, Frederic Remington.*

Cattleman's Stir-Fry Steak

1½ pound sirloin steak, cut in 1/8-inch
    thick strips
1 tablespoon paprika
2 cloves garlic, crushed
2 tablespoons butter or margarine
1 cup green onions with tops, sliced
2 green bell peppers, cut in strips
2 large fresh tomatoes, diced
1 cup beef broth
¼ cup water
2 tablespoons cornstarch
2 tablespoons soy sauce
3 cups hot cooked rice

Sprinkle steak with paprika and let set. Quickly cook steak in butter until nicely browned. Add garlic. Add onions and bell peppers, cooking until limp. Add fresh tomatoes and broth. Cover pan and simmer 15 minutes, stirring occasionally. Blend water and cornstarch; add soy sauce. Stir into steak mixture and cook until tender. Serve over hot, fluffy rice. Serves 6.

Flaming Gorge National Recreation Area is so named because of the flaming red and orange colorations in the sandstone surrounding the reservoir. The colors are those of a magnificent sunset. It is used for flood control, irrigation, fishing, camping and other water-related activities.

Rocky Mountain Trout

4 6-ounce fillets of trout (Mackinaw, rainbow
    or cut-throat)
2 tablespoons butter
1½ cups fresh lump crabmeat
1 cup sliced mushrooms
8 canned artichoke hearts, chopped
garlic powder to taste
juice of 2 lemons

Saute fish, on each side, in skillet. Remove. Place all other ingredients in skillet with remaining butter. Saute until thoroughly hot and spoon over fish. Serves 4.

Big Country Beef or Pork Ribs

14 ounces ketchup
1 onion, chopped
1 tablespoon Worchestershire sauce
dash Tabasco
salt and black pepper to taste
1 tablespoon lemon juice
2 cloves garlic, chopped
1 cup red wine vinegar
¼ cup white Karo syrup
½ cup water
6 to 8 pounds beef or pork ribs

Blend all sauce ingredients. Coat ribs generously. Bake, covered, at 350 degrees, approximately 45 minutes, turn over and bake an additional 45 minutes, or until tender.

Uncover and brown 30 minutes additionally. Serves 4.

1965 was the 75th anniversary of Wyoming Statehood

Frankfurter Crown with Potato Salad

16 frankfurters
1½ cups barbecue sauce (homemade or
bottled)
fresh parsley
potato salad

Place frankfurters in a shallow pan, top with barbecue sauce and let set 30 minutes, turning to coat. Drain and reserve sauce. Thread frankfurters through center, using heavy white string. Tie ends.

Stand frankfurters on end to form crown. Fill center with potato salad. Drizzle some barbecue sauce on frankfurters. Bake at 375 degrees for 25 minutes, basting frankfurters several times with sauce.

Lift crown carefully to a serving platter, using wide spatulas underneath crown to lift. Decorate base of crown with parsley sprigs. Remove string as you serve. Serves 8.

Potato Salad

9 medium potatoes, boiled and thinly sliced
1½ cups celery, finely chopped
3 tablespoons fresh parsley, minced
1 ounce fresh minced Spanish pimiento
6 strips crisply fried bacon, crumbled
2 tablespoons bacon drippings
2 tablespoons cider vinegar
3 tablespoons tarragon vinegar
juice of ½ lemon
salt and pepper to taste
paprika

Combine all ingredients except paprika. Fill crown and bake as directed. Dust with paprika prior to serving.

Hell's Half Acre, west of Casper, near the south fork of the Powder River, is a rugged 320-acre depression where the wind and water have worn the brightly colored sandstone and shale there into unusual gullies, ridges and spectacular towers.

Campfire Chili

2 pounds ground beef (or game or mixed)
2 medium yellow onions, chopped
3 cloves garlic, minced
oil
16-ounce can tomatoes, broken up
4 tablespoons tomato paste
4 ounces diced green chilies
2 picked jalapeno peppers, chopped (optional)
3 tablespoons chili powder
1 teaspoon each salt and cumin
1 tablespoon oregano
two 14½-ounce cans beef broth
5 cups water
15-ounce can pinto beans

Brown meat with onions and garlic in oil. Add tomatoes, tomato paste, chilies, jalapenos, seasonings, beef broth and water. Bring mixture to a boil. Reduce heat to low and cook 4 to 5 hours, stirring occasionally. Adjust seasonings, if necessary. Add beans during last 30 minutes of cooking. Serve hot in bowls with an assortment of condiments such as grated cheeses, sliced olives, Pico de Gallo, chopped onion, etc. Yield: 3 quarts.

Cheyenne Frontier Days, Wyoming's most popular annual event, which has been staged since 1897, is held the last week in July. It has been called "the daddy of them all."

Pioneer Meat and Potato Pie

4 medium potatoes, peeled and sliced
1 tablespoon butter
oil
1 medium onion, chopped
½ cup celery, chopped
pinch oregano
1 clove garlic, chopped
1 pound ground round
¼ cup green olives, sliced
8-ounce can tomato sauce
a small can mushrooms
1 cup Cheddar cheese, shredded

Butter a 13 x 9-inch casserole dish and overlap potato slices. Saute onion, celery, oregano and garlic in a small amount of oil until limp. Add meat and brown. Add olives, tomato sauce and mushrooms. Pour over potatoes, in casserole. Sprinkle with cheese and bake at 400 degrees for 35 to 40 minutes or until potatoes are done. Serves 4 to 6.

The 23,500-acre Jackson Hole Elk Refuge, established in 1912, preserves the world's largest herd of elk (or wapiti), and numbers almost ten thousand. Each autumn, the elk migrate from the snow-covered mountains of northwestern Wyoming to the refuge, where they spend the winter.

Beef or Wild Game Stew

½ pound bacon
1½ pounds lean beef chuck, buffalo, elk, deer
    or moose, cubed
16-ounce can tomatoes
6-ounce can tomato paste
2 14½-ounce cans beef broth
1 tablespoon Worchestershire sauce
1 teaspoon chili powder
2 cloves garlic, crushed
2 bay leaves
1 tablespoon fresh parsley
salt and pepper to taste
1 quart water, or more as needed
4 medium potatoes, quartered
8 small white onions, halved
8 carrots, peeled and cut in 1-inch pieces
6 stalks celery with leaves, cut in ½-inch pieces
2 cups cabbage, shredded

Chop bacon in small pieces and fry until crisp in large stew pot. Add cubed meat and brown all over. Lower heat. Add tomatoes, tomato paste, beef broth, red wine, Worchestershire sauce, seasonings and water. Simmer for one hour. Add all vegetables and more water, if needed. Stir well and cook over low heat for an additional hour or until vegetables are tender. Serves 6 to 8.

Wyoming has an abundance of magnificent wild game. It has the largest pronghorn antelope and elk herds in the world. Other big game animals include black bear, grizzly bear, mule deer, moose, mountain sheep, lynxes and mountain lions. Small game animals include beavers, badgers, martens, raccoons, foxes, coyotes, wildcats and rabbits. Game birds also abound and include ducks, geese, pheasants, sage hens, grouse and wild turkeys.

Taste of the West Casserole

1 pound ground beef
1 tablespoon oil
1 tablespoon chili powder
2 cloves garlic, minced
1 tablespoon salt
pepper to taste
1 large onion, chopped
1 green bell pepper, chopped
1 cup Rotel tomatoes with green chilies
14½-ounce can whole tomatoes
15½-ounce can kidney or pinto beans
¾ cup raw rice
14½-ounce can beef bouillon
¼ cup black olives, sliced
1 cup Cheddar cheese

Brown meat in oil. Add chili powder, garlic, salt, pepper, onions and bell pepper. Cook 3 minutes. Add tomatoes with juice, breaking up; then add beans and rice. Turn into greased 2-quart baking dish, pour beef broth over rice and meat mixture and bake, covered, at 350 degrees for 45 minutes. Sprinkle olives and cheese on top and bake, uncovered, until cheese is melted. Serves 6 to 8.

Wyoming's most important natural resources are mineral deposits, grazing land, scenery and water.

Mountain Man Zucchini-Bean Bake

2 tablespoons oil
1 cup sliced, small, tender zucchini
½ cup bell pepper, chopped
½ cup green onions with tops, sliced
¼ pound ground beef
¼ cup dry white wine
2 tablespoons tomato paste
¼ cup dark raisins
salt and pepper to taste
16-ounce can pork and beans
1 tablespoon brown sugar
1 teaspoon dry mustard (or 2 tablespoons prepared)
8-ounce package pre-sliced Cheddar cheese slices
4 slices bacon, cut in half crosswise

Heat oil in large skillet. Add zucchini, bell pepper and onion. Saute 5 minutes until tender. Add meat and brown. Stir in wine, tomato paste, raisins, salt and pepper. Cook several minutes, stirring occasionally. Add beans, brown sugar and your choice of mustard. Heat thoroughly. Fry bacon and drain.

Line each of four individual 6-ounce heat proof casseroles with a slice of cheese. Fill with bean mixture. Top each with cheese slice and two bacon slices. Heat at 400 degrees for 5 minutes, until cheese is bubbly and bacon is crisp. Yield: 4 servings.

Independence Rock is called the "Register of the Desert." Located southwest of Casper on the Sweetwater River, it is a huge granite rock, 190 feet high, with as many as 50,000 names carved, painted or scratched on its surface by those traveling west on the Oregon and Mormon Trails. Inscribed are the names of pioneers, trappers, traders, cowboys, outlaws and tourists. The early travelers tried to reach Independence Rock on July 4 and celebrations would begin with much rejoicing!

Cheesy Garden Casserole

2 cups cooked brown rice
2 cups broccoli, separated into flowerettes
1 cup carrots, sliced
1 zucchini, sliced
1 cup green beans, cut in diagonal slices
    1 inch long
2 cups Marinara sauce (homemade or bottled)
1 cup Cheddar cheese, grated
1 cup Monterey Jack cheese, grated

Place rice in oblong baking dish. Cook broccoli, carrots, zucchini and green beans separately in small amount of boiling water for 5 minutes, absorbing water.

Spoon vegetables over rice. Top with sauce. Cover and bake at 375 degrees for 30 minutes.

Combine cheeses and sprinkle over casserole. Bake 5 minutes to melt cheeses, until bubbly. Serves 6.

John D. Rockefeller Jr. Memorial Parkway is the scenic highway from Jackson that links Teton and Yellowstone National Parks. It follows the Snake River and offers fantastic views of the Grand Tetons before entering Yellowstone. It honors and immortalizes Rockefeller's important role in helping establish many national parks.

Winter Vegetable Soup (Italian Minestrone)

1 ham bone
18-ounce can tomato juice
6-ounce can V-8 juice
2 large onions, chopped
2 cloves garlic, pressed
1 teaspoon Worchestershire sauce
2 bay leaves
6 cups beef broth
2 cups of water
4 medium potatoes, diced
4 large carrots, sliced
2 stalks celery with leaves, chopped
¼ cup pearl barley
15-ounce can white (cannelonni) beans
salt and pepper to taste
⅔ cup small seashell macaroni
2 cups green cabbage, finely shredded

Combine all ingredients, except macaroni and cabbage, in large soup pot. Bring to a boil, reduce heat, cover and simmer 1½ hours until vegetables are tender. Add macaroni and cabbage and cook and additional 30 minutes. Adjust seasonings to your taste. Serves 6 to 8.

Cheyenne is one of the most historic towns in the Old West and is the state capital of Wyoming. It is also the largest city, founded in 1867 when Major General Grenville M. Dodge, chief engineer for the Union Pacific Railroad, selected the site of a new rail town. Cheyenne is called "the Magic City of the Plains." It has many fine historical museums.

Wyoming Sunset Soup

1 quart tomato juice
1 cup beef bouillon
3 whole cloves
6 fresh black peppercorns
1 bay leaf
pinch basil
1 carrot, grated
1 rib celery with leaves, chopped
2 tablespoons fresh parsley, minced
1 teaspoon onion powder
1 spiral lemon rind
1 orange, juiced
1 teaspoon Worchestershire sauce
dash cayenne pepper to taste
lemon slices, garnish
fresh parsley sprigs, garnish
vodka (optional)

In a saucepan, combine tomato juice, beef bouillon, cloves, peppercorns, bay leaf, basil, carrot, celery, parsley, onion powder, lemon rind and orange juice. Bring to a boil, reduce heat and let simmer 10 minutes. Strain. Add Worchestershire sauce and cayenne pepper to taste.

Serve in cups or mugs with a slice of lemon and fresh parsley garnish. Serves 6.

To warm you up, add a shot of vodka to each serving!

Casper is the second largest city in Wyoming, founded in 1888. Tourists visit Casper to enjoy its many recreational activities: boating, camping, fishing, hunting and winter sports. It is also a trade center for sheep and cattle ranchers and center of oil and industry.

Indian Pumpkin Soup in Pumpkin Shell

¼ cup butter
2 onions, chopped
½ cup lentils
5 cups chicken stock
1½ cups fresh cooked pumpkin, mashed
   (or canned)
1/8 teaspoon each marjoram or thyme
¼ teaspoon coarsely ground pepper
dash hot pepper sauce
1 cup half and half
½ cup fresh ham, cut in julienne strips
½ cup fresh parsley, chopped
½ cup toasted sliced or slivered almonds
pumpkin shell

In a large stockpot, melt butter. Add onions, cooking until lightly browned. Add lentils and chicken stock. Add pumpkin. Crush herbs, add to stock and add pepper and hot pepper sauce. Simmer 1½ hours. Cool. Puree. When ready to serve, heat to simmer and add half and half. Blend.

Serve in hollowed-out pumpkin. Ladle into individual soup bowls or mugs and garnish with a choice of condiments: ham, parsley and almonds. Serves 8.

Baked Goods and Desserts ...

Breads, Cakes, Pies, and Other Sweets

Abraham Lincoln Memorial Monument, Southeast of Laramie, is a large bronze bust of President Lincoln. It was completed in 1960 and marks the highest point along Interstate 80 — 8,878 feet.

Sourdough Bread

4 cups flour
2 tablespoons sugar
1 teaspoon salt
2 tablespoons oil
2 cups prepared Sourdough Starter, at
    room temperature
yellow cornmeal
egg white for glaze

Mix together flour, sugar and salt. Make a well in the center and pour in the oil. Add 2 cups of prepared Sourdough Starter and blend well with flour mixture. Dough should be soft. Knead 3 to 4 minutes on clean, floured surface.

Place dough in a greased bowl, turning to coat all dough. Cover and let rise until double in bulk. Pinch down, divide into 2 balls of dough, cover and let rest 10 minutes.

Shape dough into 2 long loaves. Sprinkle baking sheet with cornmeal and place loaves on top. Cover and allow to rise 1 hour, until double in bulk. Brush tops with egg white. Slash diagonally across tops. Bake at 375 degrees for 30 to 35 minutes, or until you feel a hollow sound when bread is thumped on top. Yield: 2 loaves.

The colorful "entertainer," America's best-known rugged frontiersman and showman of the American West, was William "Buffalo Bill" Cody. At fifteen, he made the longest ride on the Pony Express, 322 miles. He was also a buffalo hunter, supplying meat for workmen building a western railroad; this is how he got the name of "Buffalo Bill." He later became a showman and with his "Wild West Circus" he toured the United States and parts of Europe.

Sourdough Starter

2 cups flour
2 cups lukewarm water
1 yeast cake or 1 package dry yeast

Mix ingredients thoroughly in a 2-quart container of crockery, glass or plastic. Do not use metal! Cover with a double thickness of cheesecloth and store in a warm place until the "sponge" begins to bubble, rises and falls back, about 8 to 10 hours. Stir with a rubber spatula and let the mixture bubble for about 2 days. The "sponge" must "work" to achieve a thick texture and a fresh, sour aroma.

After 2 days, stir again with a rubber spatula, place a lid over the cheesecloth and store in the refrigerator. Label the container.

To replenish starter: Each time the starter is used, add equal amounts of warm water and flour. Cover with cheesecloth and allow to bubble overnight or for 6 to 8 hours, at least. Replace lid and store in refrigerator.

The town of Cody was founded in 1897. It is the home of the Buffalo Bill Historical Center and is one of Wyoming's most significant attractions. It includes four museums: Buffalo Bill Museum, Whitney Gallery of Western Art, Plains Indian Museum and Winchester Firearms Museum.

Buckskin Bread

4 cups flour
2 heaping teaspoons baking powder
1 teaspoon salt
2 heaping tablespoons shortening
1½ cups water

Sift together flour and baking powder, in a large bowl. Add salt and shortening. Mix together with your hands. Add water until dough is soft. Knead dough on floured surface. Shape into one large oblong, flat loaf.

Place on cookie sheet and bake at 350 degrees for 20 minutes. Serve hot with butter and jam. Yield: 1 loaf.

Wild Wyoming Huckleberry Muffins

2 cups flour
4 tablespoons sugar
4 teaspoons baking powder
1 cup fresh huckleberries (may substitute
blueberries)
1 egg
1 cup milk
4 tablespoons butter, melted

Sift together flour, sugar and baking powder in a bowl. Stir and pour into flour mixture. Add butter and stir until all ingredients are moistened. Pour batter into buttered muffin tins, filling one-half full. Bake at 350 degrees for 25 minutes or until done. Yield: 2 dozen.

Petroleum, natural gas and minerals make Wyoming one of the leading states in mining. Wyoming also ranks as a leader in the production of bentonite, a special clay used in oil well drilling; trona, a mineral with wide use in the chemical industry; and uranium, the raw material of atomic power.

Covered Wagon Biscuits

2 cups flour
1 tablespoon baking powder
½ teaspoon salt
⅓ cup shortening
¾ cup milk

Stir together flour, baking powder and salt. Cut in shortening with a pastry blender until crumbly. Stir quickly to incorporate just until dough follows fork around bowl. Turn out on lightly floured surface. Knead several seconds. Roll out or pat dough ½-inch thick. Cut with floured biscuit cutter and bake on ungreased cookie sheet at 450 degrees for 12 to 15 minutes. Serve piping hot. Yield: 10 to 12 biscuits.

Delicious with chokecherry syrup or huckleberry jam!

Francis Emroy Warren was one of the great cattle and sheep ranchers of Wyoming. He was elected the first state governor in 1890 but resigned to become United States senator.

Stack Cake

Stack Cake was a traditional pioneer wedding cake put together at the wedding celebration! Each guest brought a layer of cake. The layers were put together with homemade applesauce, then stacked. The bride's popularity was measured by the number of stacks she had and by the number of layers in each stack.

The cakes were usually quite colorful and flavorful, as the guests proudly showed off their baking skills with many different types of cakes being brought to the bride.

Follows is a typical six-layer molasses cake, although you may choose to vary your layers.

> **1 cup each butter, sugar and molasses**
> **3 eggs**
> **4 cups flour**
> **1 teaspoon baking soda**
> **salt to taste**
> **1 cup milk**
> **1 quart applesauce (homemade or bought)**
> **whipped cream**
> **pecans or walnuts, chopped**

Cream together butter and sugar. Fold in molasses. Add eggs, one at a time, beating to incorporate. Mix together flour, baking soda and salt. Add to creamed mixture alternately with milk, beating after each addition.

Grease and flour three 8-inch round cake pans. Fill each with 1⅓ cups batter and refrigerate remainder for three more cakes. Bake at 375 degrees for 15 minutes, or until done. Cool 5 minutes, remove from pans and cool on wire rack. Bake next three cakes.

Spread applesauce between layers. Spread top with whipped cream and nuts. Serves 24.

The White Buffalo is a rare and sacred creature. According to Indian legend, it is decreed that one day a white buffalo will lead a herd as big as the original one (60 million head) out of a cave, ready to reclaim the Great Plains.

Old Fashioned Funnel Cake

2 cups milk
2 eggs, beaten
2 cups flour
1 teaspoon baking powder
½ teaspoon salt
oil
confectioner's sugar
cinnamon

Mix milk and eggs together. Sift together flour, baking powder and salt. Pour milk mixture into flour and mix thoroughly. Test consistency of batter to determine whether it will flow properly through funnel. If the batter is too thick, add milk to thin. If batter is too thin, add flour to thicken. Heat oil in deep fryer until hot enough to fry. Pour cake batter through funnel in deep fryer. Swirl funnel around to make decorative pattern by controlling outlet with finger. Fry until golden brown and floating. Drain and sprinkle with a mixture of confectioner's sugar and cinnamon while still hot. Serve hot!

Boar's Tusk is a landmark near Rock Springs, Wyoming's largest city in the southern part of the state. The unusual rock formation was used as a landmark by early pioneers as it is hundreds of feet high and may be seen from far away.

Virginia Marks Homestead Rhubarb Pie

3 tablespoons butter
1½ cups sugar
3 cups rhubarb, chopped
3 tablespoons tapioca
1½ cups canned evaporated milk
3 beaten egg yolks
1/8 teaspoon salt
9-inch pie crust, baked
whipping cream

Combine butter, sugar and rhubarb in a saucepan. Cook slowly until tender. Add tapioca, evaporated milk, egg yolks and salt. Cook until thick. Let cool. Put into baked pie shell and top with sweetened whipped cream. Serves 6 to 8.

Harvest Pumpkin Pie

1 cup pumpkin, cooked or canned
1 pound miniature marshmallows
¼ teaspoon allspice
1 teaspoon cinnamon
½ pint whipping cream, whipped
9-inch pie crust, baked

Heat together pumpkin, marshmallows and spices, until marshmallows are melted. Remove from heat. Cool. Fold in whipped cream. Pour into pie shell. Chill until set. Serves 6 to 8.

The city of Rawlins has the distinction of being known for a paint that bears its name, "Rawlins Red." The paint pigment mines there sent the paint to New York to paint the Brooklyn Bridge when it was first constructed.

Top of the Tetons Pie

1 partially baked 10-inch pie shell
1 cup coconut flakes
1 cup semisweet chocolate chips
1 cup pecans, chopped
½ cup brown sugar
¾ cup white sugar
pinch salt
1½ tablespoons butter, melted
½ cup white corn syrup
¼ teaspoon vanilla
4 eggs, beaten

Preheat oven to 325 degrees. Toss together coconut flakes, chocolate chips and chopped pecans. Place in pie shell.

Mix together sugars, salt and melted butter. Beat in corn syrup and vanilla. Gently fold eggs into sugar mixture. Pour evenly over ingredients in prepared pie shell. Bake 55 to 60 minutes or until deep golden brown on top and nearly set in center. Cool at room temperature. Serves. 8.

1990 — Wyoming Centennial
July 10, 1890 - July 10, 1990
celebrating
100 Years of Statehood!

Cowboy Cookies

1 cup brown sugar
1 cup granulated sugar
1 cup shortening
1 teaspoon vanilla extract
2 eggs
1½ cups flour
pinch salt
1 teaspoon baking soda
3 cups rolled oats
½ cup chopped dried apricots
½ cup raisins
½ cup chopped dates
1 cup mini chocolate chips
½ to 1 cup coconut, shredded or flaked
1 mashed banana, medium

Cream together sugars and shortening. Add vanilla extract and eggs. Mix well. Blend flour, salt and soda. Add alternately with oats to sugar mixture. Stir in apricots, raisins, dates, chocolate chips, coconut and banana.

Drop by spoonfuls on ungreased cookie sheet. Bake at 350 degrees for 10 minutes or until lightly browned. Allow to cool slightly before removing.

These freeze well and are also a nutritious breakfast treat.

Index

SOMETHING SPECIAL

HOT AND HEARTY

BAKED GOODS AND DESSERTS

For additional copies of

Wonderful Wyoming
Facts and Foods

send $5.95 plus $1.50 postage and handling to:

Judy Barbour Books
2305 Park Avenue
Bay City, Texas 77414

Name _____

Address _____

City _____

State _____ Zip _____